90+ Content Ideas

FOR SOCIAL MEDIA,
BLOGS & ONLINE MARKETING

Michelle Emerson

www.michelleemerson.co.uk

Brand New Books for Authors Series

1: Finding Time to Write: How to Write More in Less Time, Embrace Your Creativity and Grab Every Opportunity to Write

2: 77 Book Marketing Ideas for Self-Published Authors on a Tight Budget

3: Publish Your Book on Kindle: From Manuscript to Published on Amazon – The Simple Step-by-Step Guide

4: Thinking of Writing a Business Book?

5: 30-Day Content Marketing Roadmap for Authors

More Books by Michelle

90+ Content Ideas for Social Media, Blogs & Online Marketing

How to Write a Brilliant Business Book

100 Positive Affirmations for Writers

Praise for the Book

This short but valuable content handbook is receiving fab reviews – here are a couple:

"One of my goals going forward is to make social media less onerous while improving my engagement with followers. Adding value rather than just spewing anything onto the page just to fill it up.

So thank you, Michelle Emerson, for your fabulous ebook - I now have approx three months of great posts! And while I have still taken up a block of time to schedule this week, it was so much easier not to have to think about it - it was all there in front of me!"

Jackie Elliott, Author and Owner of
www.sobersassylife.com

"Michelle Emerson you are a diamond, thank you! The way you word things and your prompts really work for me. Thank you."

Zahreen Sharp, Owner of
www.weddingbusinessacademy.uk

Dedication

For time-poor authors and small business owners everywhere – especially those who are regularly scratching their heads and staring into space for content inspiration.

Contents

Why Buy This Book?

Being an entrepreneur or business owner is demanding. You have to be a dab hand at all kinds of tasks. And sometimes there aren't enough hours in the day. Sometimes you can't muster up the energy to write, let alone conjure up cracking content ideas to keep your brand visible. Sometimes you feel like you've been writing the same-old vanilla-beige-bland combo forever.

And doesn't it wear you out?

Well, you can stop stressing now. I've written this book to help you create content in a timely, cool, calm way. No hair-pulling, swearing or chair-kicking necessary.

Putting your own slant on my prompts and tips means you'll find social media posts, blogs, newsletters, freebies, lead magnets, 5-day challenges, videos and mini masterclasses are way more quick and easy to create.

What's more, you'll have your own 90-day (plus) blueprint to keep you creating and posting fab content for the next quarter and the next quarter. It's so easy when you have a framework to build on.

The content marketing and repurposing strategy means you'll easily glean at least a year's worth of ideas. You'll have no more writer's block, that's for sure.

This short value-packed book is perfect for:

- **All types of business owners** who are in dire need of fresh content ideas (but can't/don't want to hire a content writer).

- **Entrepreneurs** who waste too much time staring at a blank piece of paper/white screen instead of earning money

- **Anyone** who puts off writing content until the last minute, and then wonders why they feel like giving up.

If this sounds like you, then welcome. You're about to learn the easy way to create (and repurpose) content that gets engagement and conversions, helps you connect, saves hours of your precious time, and keeps those eyes on your brand.

To get the best from this book...

Open a new Word document or Excel spreadsheet while you read and create

Storing content ideas on your PC means they are accessible and easy to reuse and reshare. (I'll talk more about repurposing later.) Monitoring engagement, views and reactions will also help you to create more of your most popular posts too and maximise these early attempts. It's time to take your content creation seriously, and I promise, when you do this, you'll reap the benefits.

NB: I've also added note sections throughout the book for you to add ideas as you go if you prefer.

Switch off the distractions

Turn off your email alerts, your social media pings and notifications. Switch off your phone – the world really doesn't end if you're unavailable for half an hour or so (I've tried it many times, and my productivity has soared). Stay focused (and hydrated too) and you'll see those new ideas come to life so quickly that you won't want to stop.

Avoid speed-reading and missing out sections

If you do this, you won't save time, because you'll have to go back and re-read the crucial points. This is a short book, anyway, so even if you're raring to spring from those starting blocks (I know you want results and quickly), please don't skip anything.

Read, write, rinse, repeat

Once your first 90+ content ideas are drafted, read through the prompts again. Round 2 of this quick and easy content creation process gets even more exciting. You'll be amazed at how many ideas you've had tucked away!

So, if you're ready, let's begin with a little preparatory work.

The Prep Work

Before you dive into the writing/creation process, you need to do some prep work.

Understanding your followers' struggles, solving their 2am panic moments and establishing yourself as a reliable, likeable, trustworthy 'go-to' expert helps you create valuable and purposeful content. And it will boost your engagement too.

There's little point creating content if you're unsure WHY you're writing, WHO you're writing for and WHAT they want to read.

Top Tip

Posting for the sake of posting (to avoid an empty page) does more damage than good. Resist the urge. Or share something newsworthy (and ethically) from an appropriate post in your social media feed instead.

Let's begin the prep work by thinking of your WHY. What's the purpose of creating content? Do you intend to:

1. Foster/build/nurture relationships?

2. Drive traffic to your website?

3. Instil the know, like and trust factor?

4. Point them towards your freebies or low hanging fruit (ie freebies, lead magnets, Facebook groups, newsletter list or low priced products/services)?

5. Build a community?

6. Get your followers onto your email list?

7. Boost your brand?

8. Demonstrate your expertise?

9. Get people to buy?

10. Something else?

_____

_____

_____

_____

_____

_____

_____

_____

_____

_____

_____

_____

_____

_____

_____

_____

_____

_____

_____

_____

_____

_____

_____

_____

_____

_____

_____

_____

_____

_____

_____

_____

_____

_____

_____

_____

Who are you writing for?

As an entrepreneur, you'll already know who your ideal client is but revisiting their profile won't do any harm.

So take some time out now to refresh your mental (or visual) image of your perfect client. If it helps, think of your favourite client or someone who ALWAYS engages with your Facebook posts. What do they respond to generally? What have been your most popular posts? What kind of people have engaged with your posts or boosted posts or adverts?

The 'Insights' tab on your Facebook page is beneficial here. Look at the stats on your other social media platforms too.

Top Tip

Whenever you write ANYTHING at all, imagine you're speaking to your perfect client on Zoom. Print out a picture of how you imagine them to look and keep it close when you're creating content.

What do they want to read?

Getting to the heart of what makes your ideal client tick already puts you a step ahead. Sharing content that plugs gaps or enhances situations is always going to get a reaction.

So think about these questions if you need to brainstorm what your followers are really looking for from your content.

- Are they struggling with something you can fix?

- Do they need motivating?

- Are they looking for inspiration to stay on their journey (eg health and wellbeing)?

- Do they want to get to know you better before they invest in your services?

- Are they looking for tips or answers?

- Are they in a particular community and just want to be able to share, see, nod and react to content that makes them tick. The writers and self-published authors who follow my social media feeds look to my posts for a book/writing/publishing/nerd/community fix that they can't always get from friends and family who aren't interested in their favourite pastime. Maybe it's the same for you?

TOP TIP

GO THROUGH YOUR POSTS AND SEE WHICH HAVE HAD THE MOST ENGAGEMENT. IF YOU FOLLOW SOMEONE ELSE IN YOUR NICHE, TAKE A LOOK AT THEIR SOCIAL MEDIA FEEDS TOO AND SEE WHAT'S BEEN GETTING THE MOST ENGAGEMENT. DON'T BE A PLAGIARIST, THOUGH! USE YOUR FINDINGS AS A SPRINGBOARD FOR YOUR UNIQUE IDEAS.

_____

_____

_____

_____

_____

_____

_____

_____

_____

_____

_____

_____

_____

_____

_____

_____

_____

_____

_____

_____

_____
_____
_____
_____
_____
_____
_____
_____
_____
_____
_____
_____
_____
_____
_____
_____
_____
_____
_____
_____
_____

Now you know WHY you're creating content, WHO you're talking to and WHAT they generally want to read, it's time to think about wowing them.

Average just doesn't cut it.

What Will Wow Your Crowd?

In this section, you're going to learn how to wow your crowd. You're going to take everything you've gleaned from your prep work and pump some steroids in.

Here's your task.

Make a list of 10 possible subjects you could write about with ease.

Here are some questions to spark ideas if you get stuck.

What is your specialist subject(s)? What topic do you know inside out and back to front that you can talk about for hours without coming up for air?

How do you help people?

What kind of products or services do you sell?

How do these help your crowd?

What are your crowd's biggest pain points?

Which keywords would people put into a Google search to find you?

What kind of results do people get from working with you?

What kind of questions do people ask you when they need your help?

Why do your current and past clients love you?

What topics do your followers connect with?

Here are my responses – maybe they'll stir up some more ideas for you.

What do you know inside out and back to front that you can talk about without drying up?

Writing – non-fiction books, marketing content, blogs, social media posts.

Proofreading – books, manuscripts, blogs.

Editing – books, manuscripts, blogs.

Publishing – on Kindle and with mainstream publishers.

Blogging. Digital marketing.

How do you help people?

Writing - I take away their pressure to create content. Mindset - I give them confidence to believe in their writing ability.

Save time - I help them leverage their time by taking care of their written content/book publishing needs.

Editing - I polish their work so it reads well and gets their message across in the best way possible.

Publishing - I help them become authors quickly and easily via Kindle.

What kind of products or services do you sell?

Online courses and programmes, 1-2-1 non-fiction book coaching, ghostwriting, editing, proofreading support and self-publishing done-for-you help.

How do these help your crowd?

Maximises their time – they can spend time writing their next book or with clients or on money-making tasks (instead of wasting hours trying to write a blog or navigate their way through the publishing process).

Speeds up their author platform / business growth.

Helps them generate regular income. Eases pressure on them – not everyone finds it easy to manage the full self-publishing process and/or create valuable content to ensure their brands stay visible.

What are your crowd's biggest pain points?

Some might struggle to write/find the right words to create good content. They may hate writing. My aspiring authors might want to write a book but don't know where to start or how to develop their outline. They lack confidence in their book idea/ability to write a book. They spend too long trying to create relevant/valuable content. They want to publish on Kindle but don't have the time/energy to do it alone or learn the process.

So from my answers, I have a pretty clear idea of what my 10 subjects are going to be:

writing

1. proofreading
2. publishing
3. editing
4. blogging
5. creating social media posts
6. writing a business book
7. digital marketing
8. newsletters
9. publishing on Kindle

Your turn!

_____
_____
_____
_____
_____
_____
_____
_____
_____
_____
_____
_____
_____
_____
_____
_____
_____
_____
_____
_____

_____

_____

_____

_____

_____

_____

_____

_____

_____

_____

_____

_____

_____

_____

_____

_____

_____

_____

_____

_____

Using Your 10 Tantalising Topics to Create All Kinds of Content

If you're struggling to find 10 tantalising topics, then just work with 5 for now. Don't waste time trying to figure out the other 5 at this stage. They will emerge naturally once you start creating your first batch of content. Promise.

Okay, so the next step is to take your 10 tantalising topics and use them to create content from 9 different angles (culminating in the 90 content ideas, which is the concept of this book).

Once you begin this process, you'll be able to come up with your prompts and create another 90 with ease.

The prompts/phrases we are going to base this content on are as follows:

- Top Tips
- The Pitfalls
- Getting Organised
- The Basics
- Targets
- Mindset
- Insider Secrets
- The Importance of
- Blocks

To let you see this in action, I've included some of the ways my 10 tantalising topics work using these prompts.

If you want to do this in the quickest and easiest way possible, just swap my subjects for yours and see how well they work.

Topic #1: Writing

- 5x **Top Tips** for Writing Every Day, No Matter What
- The **Pitfalls** Every Writer Faces & How to Overcome Them
- 3 Ways **Getting Organised** Can Boost Your Writing Output

Topic #2: Proofreading

- **The Basics** of Proofreading – What You Need to Know
- Setting Proofreading **Targets** – Why They're Crucial for Serious Authors

- 3 Ways to Change Your Proofreading **Mindset**

Topic #3: Publishing

- **Insider Secrets** From a Seasoned Kindle Publisher

- **The Importance** of Choosing the Right Publishing Platform for You

- The Biggest **Block** Stopping You From Publishing Your Book & What to Do About It.

Do you get the idea now? Excellent!

Your turn!

_____
_____
_____
_____
_____
_____
_____
_____
_____
_____
_____
_____
_____
_____
_____
_____
_____
_____

Repurposing Your 10 Tantalising Topics

I love love love repurposing content!

Squeezing every last bit of juice out of your content can shave hours off your working week. And whether you're just starting, growing your business, or taking it to six figures, you'll know how tricky it is to find the balance between making money and consistently creating content that connects and converts.

So writing something once and transforming it into all kinds of other valuable marketing is an excellent use of anyone's time. And if you start doing this, you'll quickly see what a difference it makes to your schedule. If you've got a VA, it's also a time-stealing task to delegate each month too.

Here's a list of content you'll probably need to create at some point or other in your business journey.

- Blog posts
- Guest blog posts
- Social media posts
- Video courses/series
- Podcasts
- Memes
- Online courses
- Cheat sheets
- Lead magnets
- Freebies
- Checklists
- 5-day challenges

- Ebooks
- Newsletters

Sounds like a hefty chunk of work, doesn't it? But don't worry. Because now you've got your 90+ ideas to work on, there are all kinds of magical marketing opportunities waiting for you.

Remember those examples I offered at the end of the previous chapter? Well, they could be used as stand-alone blogs, which is useful if you want to start scoping out your next 90 blogs. But did you know it's so easy to repurpose them into all kinds of other content too?

Let's talk a closer look at the 'Writing' ideas I shared with you previously.

*5x **Top Tips** for Writing Every Day, No Matter What*

This could be:

1. A stand-alone blog post - or 5x mini blog posts (1 top tip per mini blog).

2. A guest post (tweak it and add it to LinkedIn or Medium as an article, or submit it to an online magazine).

3. Social media posts for all your platforms.

4. A 1-minute video over 5 days (1 video per tip).

5. A short and sweet podcast (who says they have to be an hour long, anyway?).

6. 5 memes.

7. A short introductory course for people who want to start writing but don't know how/where to start.

8. A cheat sheet to help writers stay ahead of the game.

9. A lead magnet for unproductive writers.

10. A freebie for writers who want quick and easy tips to get them unstuck.

11. A checklist for writers who need to reign in their writing habits.

12. A 5-day challenge/free course to help writers establish a healthy/productive routine.

13. An ebook that's used as a tripwire for a more expensive product.

14. A helpful newsletter/email for your subscribers.

Oh my goodness, isn't this just fab? I've already had to stop writing and add ideas to my content journal so I don't forget them. I'm sure you have all kinds of sparks flying right now.

Looks like it's time for another notebook session!

_____
_____
_____
_____
_____
_____
_____
_____
_____
_____
_____
_____
_____
_____
_____
_____
_____
_____
_____

_____

_____

_____

_____

_____

_____

_____

_____

_____

_____

_____

_____

_____

_____

_____

_____

_____

_____

_____

If you're keen to develop this idea and repurpose as much of your content as possible, then you could try implementing the following strategy.

Decide on your theme for the month (use 1 of your 10 tantalising topics per month).

(WEEK 1)

- Write a substantial blog (1200-2k words).
- Break down that blog into 10 or 20x social media posts and 10 or 20x memes.
- Share the blogs and the posts at least two or three times a day (chances are your perfect client will catch it if you post the link more than once or twice a day at different times).

(WEEK 2)

Write a substantial blog (1200-2k words).

- Break down that blog into 10 or 20x short and sweet videos.
- Share the blogs and the posts at least two or three times a day.

(WEEK 3)

- Write a substantial blog (1200-2k words).
- Break down that blog into 10 or 20x social media posts and 10 or 20x memes.
- Share the blogs and the posts at least two or three times a day.

(WEEK 4)

- Write a substantial blog (1200-2k words).
- Break down that blog into 10 or 20x short and sweet videos.
- Share the blogs and the posts at least two or three times a day.

Having invested time at the start of each week to write blogs, you've also created enough content for:

- 40-80 social media posts
- 40-80 memes
- 40-80 short and sweet videos

All of which can be stored, scheduled and reshared again in the future.

But the most significant gain here is your blogs.

If you've written between 5k and 8k words in that first month, all with the same theme, you've created an ebook.

An ebook which could be made pretty in Canva and delivered from your website for a small fee (or a large one if you prefer).

And an ebook that could be turned into a Kindle book on Amazon. Imagine getting in front of a global audience as easily as that? For your info, this book is less than 5k words, and you can see how much value it offers. So don't be put off by thinking a Kindle book has to be 10, 20 or 30,000 words if it's going to be taken seriously. You're far better off creating regular shorter, bite-sized books that build your brand and author reputation.

Creating and sharing a monthly ebook can result in an easy passive income that continues to grow year on year. And don't worry. You'll never run out of ideas because you already have a head start!

Not bad going, really, is it?

Taking this strategy further, you could stick to it for three months and then rotate everything, so it looks like this:

August, September, October – use the strategy described previously

November, December, January – reshare the content from August, September, October (and give yourself some breathing space to focus on client work)

February, March, April – start the strategy again (with a different theme)

May, June, July – reshare the content from February, March, April (or, indeed, August, September, October) and give yourself some breathing space to earn more money.

This way, you're only actually creating content for half a year, and it's potentially going to serve you for way longer than that.

And don't worry about people seeing that you're repurposing/resharing content that you created 3/6 months earlier. No followers or subscribers have such time luxuries to notice.

Should you decide on the 'breathing space' quarter then you could play around with some of the other repurposing ideas (without the pressure).

_____

_____

_____

_____

_____

_____

_____

_____

_____

_____

_____

_____

_____

_____

_____

_____

_____

_____

On a Final Note

When it comes to creating content, please remember you need to keep in mind:

- **Who** you're writing for
- **What** they want to read
- And **Why** you're doing it.

Think about the bigger picture – even if you don't get instant reactions all of the time, don't give up. Be patient, be consistent. Play around with the timings of your posts, too.

And just because someone hasn't 'liked' your post, doesn't mean they aren't watching. I've had many authors come to me and say, "I've been watching your posts for ages, and it's like you've been reading my mind!" But their name was not familiar to me, so clearly, they hadn't been liking or sharing or commenting. The lurkers will appear when the time is right.

Remember the 80/20 rule – 80% of your content should be value, tips, help, advice and insider secrets and the other 20% can focus on sales.

No one likes being sold to all the time. Remember you're building trust and relationships and communities here, it's not about putting a price tag on your faithful social media followers, newsletter subscribers or blog readers.

The importance of engagement – just posting and running won't serve your business. You must reply to comments on your posts (social media and blogs) but have you thought about how much you engage with other people's pages? If you don't, then try to spend 15 minutes a day engaging on other posts. It can make a massive difference to your visibility. And who knows who's lurking and watching you from afar?

Always add a call to action – when you're posting on social media or publishing your blogs, try to include a call to action on everything. It could be something as simple as 'Tag a friend' or 'Comment YES if you'd like more tips like this' or 'Click here to find out more' or 'Download my free ebook'.

Want a few more content ideas? Try these:

1. Ask questions.
2. Share content from other pages (ethically, of course – don't claim the good stuff as your own).

3. Inspirational/motivation quotes – there are heaps of sites where you can find some good ones. Go for the less popular ones though if you want to avoid being a sheep.

4. Offer tips.

5. Share testimonials (social proof is always great for building up trust).

6. Share behind the scenes pictures or stories.

7. Case studies – when my client came to me with (this problem) she thought she'd never get over it but (x weeks later) and bingo!

I sincerely hope this little book has helped you see content ideas in a whole new light. Creating good stuff doesn't have to be time-consuming, and now you've got the perfect blueprint (and strategy) to build on, who knows how far it will take you?

Good luck!

Connect with Michelle

Love learning and chatting about self-publishing, writing and books? Follow me on social media for a regular fix.

www.michelleemerson.co.uk

www.facebook.com/selfpublishingservicesUK

www.linkedin.com/in/selfpublishingservicesuk

Michelle

PS: If this book has given you some new ideas and/or made you see how beneficial content marketing could be for your author business, then please leave a review on Amazon or on my LinkedIn/Facebook profiles.

You would make me so happy. ☺

About Michelle

Michelle lives in beautiful Co Durham, England, with her family and their bossy Shih Tzus, Buddy and Milo.

She's been passionate about writing since the age of 7 when Father Christmas gifted her a Victoria Plum Secret Diary and has worked in publishing since the 1990s (before indie authors were even a thing!).

If she's not locked in her office/writing cave, you'll find her out walking with her Shih Tzus, running with her sister, or in a local café eating carrot cake and drinking a chai latte.

_____

_____

_____

_____

_____

_____

_____

_____

_____

_____

_____

_____

_____

_____

_____

_____

_____

_____

_____

_____

_____

_____

_____

_____

_____

_____

_____

_____

_____

_____

_____

_____

_____

_____

_____

_____

_____

_____

_____

_____

_____

_____

_____

_____

_____

_____

_____

_____

_____

_____

_____

_____

_____

_____

_____

_____

_____

_____

_____

_____

_____

_____

_____

_____

_____

_____

_____

_____

_____

_____

_____

_____

_____

_____

_____

_____

_____

_____

_____

_____

_____

_____

_____

_____

_____

_____

_____

_____

_____

_____

_____

_____

_____

_____

_____

_____

_____

_____

_____

_____

_____

_____

_____

_____

_____

_____

_____

_____

_____

_____

_____

_____

_____
_____
_____
_____
_____
_____
_____
_____
_____
_____
_____
_____
_____
_____
_____
_____
_____
_____
_____

_____
_____
_____
_____
_____
_____
_____
_____
_____
_____
_____
_____
_____
_____
_____
_____
_____
_____
_____

_____

_____

_____

_____

_____

_____

_____

_____

_____

_____

_____

_____

_____

_____

_____

_____

_____

_____

_____

Made in the USA
Middletown, DE
12 July 2023